NEVADA'S

# VALLEY OF FIRE

by G. William Fiero

Dr. Fiero, former Professor of Geology at the University of Nevada, Las Vegas, is a graduate of Dartmouth College and completed his graduate studies at the University of Wyoming and the University of Wisconsin. Bill has had a lifelong interest in natural history and has traveled throughout North America and other continents to study and interpret geology and the natural sciences. He is well known and highly respected for his geological research and for his teaching activities, which include an extensive commitment to the education of non-scientists interested in learning more about the natural world.

*Edited by Mary Lu Moore; Book Design by K. C. DenDooven*

*Front cover: Rainbow Vista area by Ed Cooper; inside front cover: Elephant Rock, title page: Arch by Willard Clay; Pages 2 and 3: Sandstone rock outcrop by Jeff Gnass.*

Published by KC Publications in cooperation with Nevada Natural History Association

Sixth Printing, 1991 • Revised Edition



LC 84-52882. ISBN 0-916122-17-4.

*Valley of Fire is a vivid land of bold cliffs of red and white sandstone set in the midst of the grandeur that is the Mojave Desert. The stories of powerful earth forces, adapting life forms, and early man are all revealed in this unique parkland.*

# *From an Ancient Sea— A Valley of Fire*

The earliest stories of the region occupied by Valley of Fire are unrecorded in the pages of geologic history. Nowhere in the park are the earliest rocks exposed. The oldest rocks on earth date back slightly in excess of 4 billion years, but the oldest rock in Valley of Fire is about 600 million years. A youngster, indeed.

By studying surrounding areas, however, we can observe and decipher rocks that date back well over a billion years and get clues to the earliest events that may have been taking place in Valley of Fire.

Far to the north, in northwestern Utah, we can find the oldest rocks of the region. In age these *metamorphic* rocks, changed by high heat and pressure from preexisting rocks, are in excess of 2 billion years. They were, at that time, near the southern margin of the North American continent, and our area was a part of a sea floor.

The sea floor subsequently moved northward against the continent. Islands, oceanic rises, and perhaps even pieces of other continents, were carried along on the moving sea floor. This giant conveyor belt crushed its cargo against the southern part of the continent. The sweepings of the oceanic plate today comprise the oldest rocks we have yet studied in the southern Nevada region. These rocks date about 1.7 billion years old. These ancient rocks have been altered through time into metamorphic rocks. Some molten material intruded and cooled within the metamorphic rocks of the islands. In all probability, they underlie Valley of Fire.

BRUCE KAPLAN

The North American continent grew by such accretion. But what is geologically given can also be geologically removed. Sometime around a billion years ago, a thermal swelling lifted a large north-south welt through the newly sutured continent. Well to the east of Valley of Fire this uplift ruptured and ripped apart the continent. The rift tore in a northerly direction approximately through the central part of the state of Nevada. Slowly the western fragment drifted away from North America. The rift filled with dark, heavy, hot, molten material from below the crust. Seawater flooded onto the low-lying heavy rocks of the rift, and a new ocean formed. The western fragment of North America is probably lodged into what is now Asia and composes a portion of central Siberia.

*Tilted sandstone rocks are modified into graceful shapes by the geologic processes of erosion. Water is the most active erosive agent, even here in the desert. It couples with the enormity of geologic time to achieve its artistic results.*

The thermal swelling along the edge of the old rift margin slowly contracted as the heat from below subsided. Gradually, the continental margin of the new ocean sank below sea level. Marine waters flooded over the contracted, sunken continental edge, and the ocean covered Valley of Fire. In southern Nevada we were not a part of an oceanic plate but rather a submerged portion of the foundered continental edge.

Standing outside the visitor center, scanning the dry, hot desert floor to the west, one finds it difficult to visualize this earliest recorded geologic history of Valley of Fire. Almost 600 million years ago the sea invaded this area. Its shimmering waters were hundreds of feet deep and extended from horizon to horizon. Myriads of animals and plants thrived in the warm waters, life forms that gradually evolved in complexity over

WILLARD CLAY

the 300 million years the sea covered the region. Simple worms and jellyfish yielded space to complex fish and clams.

Life adapted explosively to this fertile environment, and virtually every niche was occupied by living creatures. Occasionally the sea would retreat, leaving piles of discarded shells and vast limy mudflats to dry, crack, and harden under the warm sun. But for most of this great span of time (the *Paleozoic,* or "old-life," era), our present desert existed as the watery world of the ocean.

Thick piles of lime muds and shells were deposited, layer upon layer. Each change in environment—sea temperature, chemistry, or water depth—would leave its mark as a distinct bed of limestone or its close relative dolostone. These accumulated deposits of marine origin would ultimately bury this part of Nevada with carbonate sediments several miles thick.

The best exposures of these ancient sediments are in the southern part of Valley of Fire. An example is the high ridge that fills the skyline across the valley south of the visitor center. The gray rocks of the Muddy Mountains are the limy graveyards of countless living creatures of the ancient sea. These ancient limestones may also be seen along the road into the park from Interstate 15.

### The Land Rises

About 200 million years ago the sea floor slowly rose. The oceanic plate to the west of North America began to move obliquely against the continent. These powerful forces to the west lifted the land near Valley of Fire. As the water became progressively more shallow, fine muds were washed in from emerging land areas. The sea floor, formerly blanketed by lime deposits and shells, became more muddy and sandy. The shallower water was more susceptible to rapid temperature and salinity changes. Currents and waves often roiled the shallow bottom. Life forms that had adapted to the deeper marine waters could no longer tolerate the new conditions, and worms and clams that favored sandy conditions were left to occupy the shallow waters.

*Gray limestones of the Muddy Mountains act as a backdrop to the red sandstones of Valley of Fire. The limestones, deposited in an ancient sea, contrast with younger sandstones, remnants of an enormous sandy desert. This is a land of geologic contrasts.*

Eventually the sea retreated totally from the region, and the water-saturated, ripple-marked muds dried and cracked in the warm, sunny climate. Rains dimpled the mud surface; their impressions, together with mud cracks and ripple marks, are to be found in the rocks today. Sluggish streams crossed the terrain, depositing veneers of coarser sand on the mudflats. Occasional downpours swelled the drainages to torrents, and coarser gravels washed down from distant highlands. These floodwaters often carried twigs, branches, and logs of trees similar to the conifers of today.

Some of the logs buried by mud were slowly altered with a molecule-by-molecule replacement of woody materials by quartz and other minerals to become the petrified logs of today. Exposure of sediments to air caused many of the iron compounds in the sands and muds to oxidize and form rust. Reds, purples, lavenders, and pinks dominate the color of these former muds and sands. Geologists call these deposits the Moen-

BILL FIERO

*A geologic moment ago, this petrified log was buried. In another geologic eye blink it will be gone. Woody materials of the log were replaced by quartz and other minerals. Earth movements fractured the petrified logs, and desert storms have scattered the fragments.*

BILL FIERO

*A rainstorm of more than 150 million years ago is recorded in the pocked shale surface. The raindrop impressions are so clear that the ancient storm seems to have just occurred. Rocks retain records of past events that are as easy to read as a history book if the observer has some geologic knowledge.*

kopi, Shinarump, and Chinle formations. These rock names are derived from localities on the Navajo Reservation to the east, where the beds are clearly exposed.

Few fossils are to be found in these beds, as the oxygenated environment caused rapid decomposition of plants and animals. Some footprints and bones of dinosaurs and other reptiles have been discovered in other locations, such as the area to the northeast of the Grand Canyon. Petrified wood is the most common fossil remnant in southern Nevada.

These sand, gravel, and mud formations are common in Valley of Fire. Most of the valley occupied by the primary east-west road in the park contains these deposits. Because they are soft they erode easily, and most of the lowlands in the park show exposures of these beds. These deposits are of *Mesozoic* ("middle-life") age. During the nearly 75 million years that the mud-sand conditions prevailed, approximately 4,500 feet of these deposits were plastered over the limestones of Valley of Fire.

The gypsum deposited in these beds by the drying seas has created a problem for administrators of the park. Groundwater is saturated with these soluble salts, creating a hardness and salinity in some areas almost comparable to seawater. Water is a precious item at Valley of Fire, and everyone needs to make an effort to conserve it for future use.

## The Desert That Was

Anyone visiting the park at midday in summer scarcely needs a reminder of the awesome power of the desert. The searing heat and lack of water seem almost unbearable. But in ages past, the Valley was subjected to desert conditions even more demanding on life than the desert of today. For tens of millions of years the area that is now the park was a barren desert covered by lofty sand dunes. Wind carved and swirled the sands into fantastic formations of multi-angled layers. Thousands of feet of sand piled up in the region, carried there by winds from the erosion of distant highlands.

*Tilted shales of the Mesozoic Era dominate the landscape of lower areas of the park. The pale reddish, purple, and brown hues result from oxidation of iron-bearing minerals. These ancient muds settled from slow-moving rivers and along mud flats bordering the sea. It was a different environment then—only a few degrees north of the equator, with warm and humid air. Early dinosaurs walked these muds.*

K. C. DENDOOVEN

*A great sandy desert covered much of the southwestern portion of the continent 140 million years ago. Vast spans of geologic time carved the tilting layers of this ancient sand dune into sharp relief. Evidence of shifting winds of long ago is revealed by erosion. This Saharan environment is beautifully preserved in the Aztec sandstone in the park.*

ED COOPER

Today, almost a half-mile thick, these "fossil" dunes comprise the beautifully shaped red and white sandstone bluffs, the most scenic aspects of Valley of Fire. The perfectly preserved swirled layers of wind-blown sand illustrate a page of Mesozoic history more than 140 million years old. This sandstone, termed Aztec sandstone by geologists, extends over large areas of the Southwest. The great towers and cliffs of Zion National Park in Utah and of Red Rock Canyon west of Las Vegas, Nevada, are carved from this formation. Some fragments of dinosaur remains have been found elsewhere in this bed, but the fossil record is sparce as a result of the oxygen-rich environment.

The sandstone varies in color from deep reds and purples to tans and whites. Delicate and subtle changes in tones are thought to be the result of groundwater percolating through the sand and leaching the oxidized iron. By tracing individual layers of sandstone one can follow the paths of ancient, slow-moving subterranean waters. The passage of these waters altered and transformed the chemistry of mineral grains. The result is a pleasing, artistic intermingling of colors.

K. C. DEN DOOVEN

*Erosion seeks weakness in stone. The sandstone layers have soft interbeds allowing erosive forces to erode differentially. Holes form where the rock is especially vulnerable. Fanciful forms result from the probing agents of the weather.*

In some parts of the park, such as the areas near the visitor center and near Atlatl Rock, the rocks are a deep red color. Moving toward White Domes, the intergrading of colors occurs gradually, until the sandstone becomes almost uniformly white in the area of the domes.

### The Earth Moves

The land rises in response to thermal nudges from deep below the crust. In the magmatic interior of the earth the driving heat engine creates large swirling currents. These slow-moving convective movements impinge against the thin skin of hard surface crust. The surface yields to such gargantuan pressures by moving. As the crust shifts, large pieces called *plates* move en masse.

Some of the plates pull apart from each other. Such divergent motion creates large rifts in the crust. These rifts are rapidly filled with *magma* from below. These molten materials have a deep source. They are heavy, fluid, and usually black. They sink low into the underlying magmas and become topographically low regions of the earth's surface. The water that falls onto the crust runs down into these low areas. Through the millennia of the earth's early history they gradually filled with water. They are the ocean basins of our planet.

Other plates are composed of lightweight silica-rich rocks that floated to the surface during the earliest days of the earth's history. This light-colored silicate scum contains the oldest rocks on earth. They are the continents.

When plates move toward each other the heavy ocean-floor plates are forced under the lighter-weight continents. Such *subduction* into the Stygian depths below the massive continents heats the oceanic plates. Eventually the ocean plates melt. But before they are destroyed, they heave upward from below the continents. The land surface above buckles and is thrust up. Also, as the lightweight portion of the heavy plate melts it forces magma upward into the overlying continent. These magmas often break through at the surface as volcanos. They become saturated with silica as they penetrate the continent. Such an

WILLARD CLAY

alteration of chemistry creates magmas that are sticky and viscous. The plumbing of these volcanos is constantly becoming clogged; thus they are explosive.

During late Mesozoic time, the sea-floor plate that lay beneath the Pacific Ocean to the west of the North American continent was moving directly against the continent. The heavy oceanic plate was forced below North America. It created titanic compressive forces as it resisted subduction. The melting plate also injected its lighter-weight components upward into the continent as huge magmatic intrusive bodies. Cooled remnants of these *igneous* intrusions comprise the core of the Sierra Nevada Mountains today. These large granitic intrusions forced their way up into the crust and shoved aside the existing continental rocks as they forcefully injected themselves upward. Such intrusive activity redoubled the compressive forces on the crust of the western United States.

In Valley of Fire the earth responded to the inexorable pressures that resulted from these far-off events. A large belt of earth movement extended from southern Nevada northward to Canada. The rocks to the west were shoved eastward, sliding atop one another like a massive deck of cards. This zone of movement is referred to as the Sevier Orogenic belt. Compression created huge faults and large areas of folded rocks. Two major compressive faults of this Sevier movement lie in or adjacent to Valley of Fire.

*Late evening light casts deep shadows into the rugged landscape of the park. The contrasts of this wild and beautiful landscape are more clearly etched at this time. Earth tones in the tilted red and white sandstones seem to vibrate with the intensity of the last rays of the sun. Distant mountains stand in parched and wrinkled folds against the sky. The thrilling call of a canyon wren pierces the desert silence, and the ravens return on whistling wings to roosts in the shadowed holes in the canyon walls. Another night descends upon the park.*

*The gray limestone beds of the Paleozoic sea stand in relief against the skyline. They tower over the red desert sandstones of the younger Mesozoic time. Tremendous earth forces have heaved the millions of tons of ancient gray rock over the younger sandstones. In Valley of Fire titanic forces have shifted the earth's crust.*

*Winter is a special time to visit the park. The silence is profound. The Virgin Mountains, powdered with snow, form a backdrop to the rugged landscape of Valley of Fire. The visitor center appears to huddle within the sheltered confines of rock.*

*The cross-beds of fossil sand dunes have been revealed by erosive scour. Winds, about 140 million years ago, gently blew sand grains up the gradual slope of a dune. The grains tumbled down the steep face sloping away from the wind. As the winds shifted direction, the old dune geometry was dissected and new dune shape formed. The cross-beds give a pleasing sculpted appearance to the outcrops.*

These mountain-building forces in what is now the park area first occurred after deposition of the Aztec sandstone. The exact time of this event is not known, but it was probably close to 100 million years ago. From Atlatl Rock through the valley south of the visitor center to the east entrance of the park, the land was upwarped into a major fold. Seen to the east of the visitor center, this upwarp, termed an *anticline,* tilted the rocks toward the east. Rocks on the western side of the valley were canted to the west. Like a large inverted spoon, the anticline slopes downward to Lake Mead. The resistant Aztec sandstone was upwarped along this fold into a large hill. But with the passing of time, erosion has removed the highest part of the Aztec, exposing the soft shales of the Chinle formation below the sandstone. These muds were vulnerable to erosion, and a broad valley now occupies the apex of the upwarp.

Response to crustal pressures not only yielded large folds but also created faults of great magnitude. These great rifts in the crust must have generated massive earthquakes in the region. Compressional forces crushed the rocks together. Release was ultimately found by the shoving of large segments of rock up at a low angle and over younger sediments.

Such movement, termed *thrust faulting,* forced the old marine limestone of the ancient sea over the sand-dune deposits of the Aztec sandstone. The old gray limestones were pushed a minimum distance of 14 miles toward the north, and the total thrusting may have forced the rocks tens of miles over the Aztec. This large fault is known as the Muddy Mountain thrust. It was originally mapped by a well-known geologist, Dr. Chester Longwell.

Looking to the south of the visitor center, one can see the high gray limestone ridges of the Muddy Mountains, representative of the upper portion of the thrust fault. The incredible forces necessary to move large segments of the crust such distances make human power seem small indeed. The uplifted highland shed erosional gravels; these are found today in the eastern part of the park.

Continued pressure created a major, almost vertical, fault that lifted rocks of the Muddy Mountains thousands of feet upward, placing the marine limestones adjacent to the upper part of the Aztec sandstone. This major fault, named the Arrowhead fault, extends east-west along the south side of the valley occupied by the visitor center and Atlatl Rock. The gray limestones, first shoved northward by the Muddy Mountain thrust, were broken and uplifted by the high-angle Arrowhead fault. The trace of the fault where the gray limestones abut the red Aztec sandstones can be clearly seen to the south of the visitor center.

Along the Arrowhead fault some movement has been documented that attests to a lateral shearing (the side-by-side movement of crustal blocks). In this manner the Muddy Mountain region was shifted eastward relative to Valley of Fire, probably at a more recent time.

*Gravels once buried the sandstone formations in Valley of Fire. The surrounding Muddy Mountains, uplifted by faults, towered thousands of feet above the sandstone. Erosion scoured down the highland, and vast gravel aprons of debris buried the surrounding rock. But erosion is both a giver and a taker. Later erosion stripped the gravel veneer, leaving only remnants capping mesas in the eastern part of the park.*

Following the formation of the Muddy Mountain and Arrowhead faults, perhaps as recently as 70 million years ago, an even larger thrust fault, the Glendale thrust, moved another segment of the crust up and over the gray limestones of the Muddy Mountain thrust block. Evidence for this thrusting occurs primarily to the north of the park. This thrust overturned portions of the block below and created a series of subsidiary vertical faults and thrust sheets. Renewed folding of the major anticline of Valley of Fire may have occurred at this time.

Evidence of these subsidiary faults may be observed within the park. The east side of the Aztec sandstone at Atlatl Rock is bounded by a high-angle fault. The sandstones have been dropped down along the Atlatl fault. From Atlatl Rock picnic area one can see the Aztec sandstone at the petroglyph site and, immediately to the east and at the same level, the muds of the older Chinle formation. West of the large sandstone bluffs of Atlatl Rock, coarse gravels have been down-dropped against the Aztec along the high-angle, northwest-trending Camp fault.

The highland uplifted by the Glendale thrust shed large amounts of gravel. The remnants of this large alluvial fan, called the Overton fanglomerate, lie in the easternmost part of the park and cap several large mesas.

The *Cenozoic* ("recent-life" era) extends back 70 million years from the present. During this time earth movements have continued to frac-

GAIL BANDINI

*A ladder, designed to blend with the rock, leads visitors to a close-up view of Indian artwork carved into dark patinas covering the rock surface.*

BILL FIERO

ture and deform the rocks of this region. A major lateral fault, the Las Vegas shear zone, has been traced through the area to the south of the park. Movements of as much as 40 miles of lateral shearing have been described. These faults, similar in nature to the San Andreas or Garlock faults in California, probably reactivated some of the earlier faults of Valley of Fire.

A region just to the east of Valley of Fire and other areas of southern Nevada were downwarped into large closed basins by earth movements. As the waters trapped in them slowly evaporated, these Cenozoic basins became the site for the formation of salts. Magnesite, borates, and lithium-rich sediments are found in these basins adjacent to the park.

The beautiful rock formations of Valley of Fire have been created largely by the fracturing of the Aztec sandstone. Not all fractures had fault movement. Brittle old sand dunes responded to earth pressures by cracking without movement. Such fractures are called *joints.* The present vertical faces of many of the sandstone bluffs are the result of the collapse of blocks of sandstone along vertical cracks.

ED COOPER

*Framed by a whimsical arch of Mesozoic sandstone, gray limestones of the earlier Paleozoic sea fill the skyline. Compressional forces uplifted the old beds into the Muddy Mountains.*

GAIL BANDINI

*Picnic areas and campgrounds are hidden among the recesses of sandstone outcrops. Here one finds privacy and the opportunity to share a quiet time with the natural world of rocks, plants, birds, lizards, and ground squirrels. The sloping rock surfaces become natural playgrounds for children and adults. The rocks tempt one's imagination (and feet) into exploring this world of shape and form.*

*The flow of rock reflects the flow of time. Wrinkled, etched, and scoured by time, ancient rock walls stand exposed to the inexorable eroding forces of water and wind. Melting snow and rainwater percolate downward through the sandstone. The water dissolves the cementing carbonate and iron from between the grains of sand, weakening the structure. Grain by grain the rock disintegrates. As the water emerges along exposed rock faces it evaporates into the dry desert air, leaving behind a residue of iron to veneer the rock with a dark brown or black patina of desert varnish.*

## The Rocks Today

Deposition of limestones, shales, and sandstones created many diverse materials ideal for the sculptor. Earth movements arranged these materials in an interesting manner, resulting in folds, faults, and joints. But the beauty seen in the rocks of Valley of Fire is chiefly the result of that great sculpturing process of geology—erosion.

Chemical erosion has altered original materials and created brilliant colors in the rocks. The addition of reds by rusting iron minerals, the creation of white sandstones by the leaching out of iron, and the mixing of all shades on the palette of chemical change have resulted in the colorful diversity we see today.

Chemical action has added soluble materials—lime and silica—to the groundwater. Moving through the joints and fault surfaces of Aztec sandstone, these chemicals occasionally find an environment for precipitation. The joints are sometimes filled with these chemicals. After precipitation the newly formed minerals of calcite or

*Nature is the master sculptor.* *Rock, one of the hardest substances in the natural world, is gently shaped and molded into fanciful forms and shapes by water, one of the most pliable and flexible substances. Out of such a paradox is created beauty. Dark and light contrast to highlight the sculpted forms. Internal structure and layering of the rock add a delicate flow to the external structure. Inner dimensions of the rocks' memory of long-past events control and shape the present outline of the eroding remnants of the past.*

DAVID MUENCH

JEFF GNASS

*Rock defies destruction, but this is an illusion of permanence. Time is the most powerful and subtle of nature's tools. We see an instant of time—one frame in a continuum of the millenia. A moment earlier the scene was different; a moment later it will be gone.*

K. C. DENDOOVEN

*Cementation focuses around a nucleating point such as a quartz crystal or an iron grain. The binding carbonate then grows outward in spherical shells from this point. Freed by erosion at the surface, these hardened spheres weather out as "Indian marbles."*

quartz, often harder than the surrounding sandstone, are left standing as narrow ridges after the sandstone has eroded away. Where blocks have sheared off, the vertical joints thus exposed are often veneered with the white mineral deposits.

Other joint surfaces are coated with a black substance. This "desert varnish" results from chemical action, perhaps further modified by microscopic plants. Leached from the rocks by the movement of water, iron and manganese are deposited on the rock surface as water emerges and evaporates over thousands of years. These blackened surfaces were favored by the first inhabitants of the Valley of Fire as ideal sites for carving rock art.

Both groundwater and rainwater are constantly dissolving the cement between sandstone grains of the Aztec. Due to variations in permeability, the original cementation was discontinuous and irregular. As a consequence some parts of the sandstone are more readily attacked by water, Holes and hollows in the sandstone result, making the Aztec a natural playground for children.

Some particularly well-cemented parts of the sandstone have resisted chemical destruction by water; knobs, ridges, and fins are the results.

*The "Seven Sisters" shelter picnics from the desert sun and wind. These erosional remnants have near-vertical faces, resulting from collapse along fractures in the brittle sandstone. We can speculate about future shapes by observing cracks in the existing forms.*

Small knobs sometimes weather free from the sandstone, leaving round "Indian marbles" at the base of the bluffs.

Sand grains released from the cemented formation are blown into small dunes, which then create ecological habitats for many desert plants and animals. They give the curious visitor the opportunity to compare the ancient "fossil dunes" of the Aztec with modern dunes.

The park is noted for its many diverse and whimsical formations: an elephant, a duck, beehives, the "Seven Sisters," and as many varied creatures as imagination can create. Most of these features are the result of chemical sapping of cemented rock aided by the natural breakage planes of joint and bedding surfaces.

Contrary to common belief, wind has not been as active an erosion agent within the park as has water. Chemical dissolution, freezing and thawing with resultant expansion in joint surfaces, and the effect of the raindrop give water more importance than wind as an erosive force. Anyone who has witnessed the intensity of a desert thunderstorm and the power of a flash flood following it can attest to the carrying strength of water in the desert. Lack of extensive vegetation results in large amounts of erosion during floods.

Windblown sand does modify the park, however. Throughout the park wind-polished stones, or *ventifacts*, can be found on the ground. Wind also distributes fine sand particles, heaping them into small dunes on the lee sides of ridges and sweeping other surfaces clean of all sand, leaving a gravel cover known as "desert pavement."

Hundreds of millions of years have witnessed the creation and modification of the materials that have made Valley of Fire one of the most geologically interesting and scenic areas in Nevada. Preservation of this unique area for future generations to appreciate in its natural state is a challenge to the sensitivity and responsibility of every traveler in this geological wonderland!

## SUGGESTED READING


Fiero, G. William. *Geology of the Great Basin.* Reno: University of Nevada Press, 1985.

Longwell, Chester R. *Structure of the Northern Muddy Mountain Area, Nevada.* Geological Society of America Bulletin, Volume 60. Boulder, Colorado: 1949.

Longwell, Chester R., et al. *Geology and Mineral Deposits of Clark County, Nevada.* Nevada Bureau of Mines, Bulletin 62. Reno: University of Nevada, Mackay School of Mines, 1965.

Shelton, John S. *Geology Illustrated.* San Francisco: W. H. Freeman, 1966.

K. C. DENDOOVEN

# *Adaptations to the Desert*

Human beings survived through thousands of years in this desert region by adaptation and ingenuity, yet they in turn were dependent upon adaptations that evolved through millions of years before they arrived. What of the plants and animals on which man depended and still depends? What are their ingenious methods of survival?

The techniques of survival in the desert are

linked within this desert ecosystem. Plants and animals have unique and interesting strategies, but both must operate within the controls imposed on them by climate and geology.

Valley of Fire occupies a portion of the Mojave Desert. This region is characterized by cold winters and hot, dry summers. Rainfall is not only sparse but also widely scattered. One part of the park may have prolific spring flowers in response to local rains, and the rest of the area may have no flowering plants at all. Scientists have determined that most annual plants require about an inch of rain during October and November to trigger germination. Excess rain promotes even more luxuriant growth. However, if there is an early freeze, autumn rains may not penetrate the

DAVID MUENCH

*A beavertail cactus in a dry wash defies erosion. The taller shrubs are creosote bush, a dominant plant in the Mojave Desert. The low shrub, bursage, is so often found with creosote bush that this plant assemblage is referred to as the creosote-bursage community.*

soil, and desert conditions will prevail. In other words, the trigger pulled in fall determines the flowering conditions for spring.

The geologic substrate dictates the local environment for a plant. Seeds may fall on bare rock, or sand, or perhaps muds. Each species must devise methods of coping with these differing conditions.

Valley of Fire offers a unique opportunity to study plants. Although the park is a part of the Mojave Desert, it is on the edge of other major plant assemblages. Representatives of these other dramatically different plant types are mingled in a fantastic variety. Mojave Desert plants, adapted to survival primarily in the hot deserts of the Southwest, are abundant. The ever-present creosote bush, bursage, and brittlebush are representative of this group.

Mixed with the hot-desert plants are Great Basin varieties commonly found to the north or at higher elevations. This group can adapt to cold conditions as well and includes purple sage, black brush, and banana yucca. Some species have adapted to the cold climates and sandy soils of the Colorado Plateau to the east and are found at the edge of their range in Valley of Fire. Sandy soils derived from Aztec sandstones are suitable for these hardy plants: Spanish bayonet, with its long spearlike leaves, and Mormon tea.

### Plant Strategies for Survival

Rigors of the desert have required unique adaptations by its inhabitants. The hot sun and infrequent rains are conditions that must be reckoned with if a species is to survive.

The creosote bush has reduced its exposure to the sun by reducing its own leaf size. To minimize the heat of direct sunlight the leaves are often oriented vertically, and the resinous coating of the leaves prevents excessive loss of water. This ingenious shrub, one of the most widespread in Valley of Fire, has also developed a form of chemical warfare. It produces an antibiotic within its roots that permeates the soil and inhibits the growth of competitors.

Some plants have developed the ability to store water during frequent periods of drought. Cacti and yucca have extensive, shallow root systems designed to capture all the water they can possibly absorb from the infrequent rains. They store rainwater in their fleshy tissues. To minimize water loss these plants assume a spheroidal shape that lowers the amount of surface area while at the same time maintains maximum volume for storage capacity. There is a hazard, however, to being a succulent in a desert; animals relish the juicy tissues. But these resourceful plants have adapted yet a step further to reduce this threat to their existence. They have developed numerous spines to discourage would-be diners of the animal kingdom!

*Preceding pages: The red and white tilted Mesozoic sandstones, with the gray Paleozoic marine limestones as a backdrop, typify Valley of Fire. Photo by Ed Cooper.*

JEFF GNASS

*Low sunlight highlights the silver cholla's spines. An animal nudging the cholla is quickly impaled on the spines, which are firmly fixed to the plant. This defense protects the plant's precious water from potential munchers. Also, as the animal retreats, a nodule of the plant remains affixed to the hapless creature. When this nodule is kicked, picked, or flicked off, it falls to the ground and quickly roots in the soil. Another cholla is born.*

Water is usually abundant in the desert, but it lies tens or hundreds of feet beneath surface sands. This permanent source of water is tapped by another group of plants: *phreatophytes* (free-AT-o-fights), or "pump-plants," that have developed deep root systems. These plants, such as mesquite and desert willow, have not developed the succulent habit of their neighbors because water storage for them is unnecessary. They have a long life span in which to grow and extend their roots into the deep water beneath the water table. In winter they drop their leaves, perhaps to protect themselves from frost. Temperatures are often too low for effective photosynthesis, so they minimize risk by drawing their resources from the leaves into their woody stems.

The most elaborate and commonly used strategy to avoid drought has been developed by desert annuals such as primroses and sunflowers. Since each plant has but one opportunity to reproduce, these plants take the greatest gamble of all. If conditions aren't right, they don't even try!

For most plants the seed stage is the most drought-resistant period. The next stage, the seedling, is usually the stage most vulnerable to drought. The annual must make this transition under optimum conditions in order for the individual and the species to survive.

How does the seed determine the right time to germinate? Annual plants in more humid environments are triggered by temperature and moisture conditions in the soil. A warmer temperature alone could be disastrous for a desert plant. A brief desert shower might increase moisture level in the soil for just a short time, causing the plant to germinate, only to encounter extreme drought caused by rapid evaporation. Desert annuals, therefore, have evolved elaborate techniques to maximize chances of survival.

Some desert annuals have devised a strategy utilizing a growth inhibitor within the seed coat. This substance must be washed off before the seed can germinate, a process that requires many periods of wetting from desert storms. The seed, in a sense, is monitoring the long-term environment. After rainfall has been sufficient for its needs, it quickly germinates, utilizing soil moisture. Thickness of the inhibitor varies from seed to seed in one species, with the result that the

Ancient sand dunes erode into modern sandy areas as the materials of nature recycle. These porous soils are favored by annual plants like the white dune primrose and the yellow Parry tack-stem. In early spring, flowers often bloom profusely beneath the sand cliffs. The sweetness of their aroma is certainly not wasted on the desert air; it can be detected for miles.

K. C. DENDOOVEN

Desert storms are rare, but occasionally torrents of water rush down the washes. The resulting gravel and concentrated moisture support a unique community of generally larger plants such as this indigo bush.

K. C. DENDOOVEN

Clay soils, derived from eroded shales of ancient sediments, support another unique plant community. The fine texture and high gypsum content of these soils are challenges to the ingenuity of plants. Desert annuals dot the soil surface in spring. Hardy perennials, such as desert holly, evolve special adaptations to survive in this environment. Coarse-textured leaves covered with fine hairs reduce water loss by decreasing wind velocities across leaf surfaces.

# Plant Communities

*Plants are extremely sensitive indicators of their desert environments. Different soil types are reflected by unique species adapted to varying conditions. Differing amounts of water, sun exposure, or temperature changes can also be detected. Plants, therefore, naturally group into communities according to their requirements.*

K. C. DENDOOVEN

Bare rock surfaces, the most rigorous of habitats, are home to a highly specialized plant community. Thrusting their roots deep into crevices and cracks in the rocks, these plants utilize all available soil and moisture. Rock nettle, with its countless small, sharp hairlike needles covering broad green leaves, shares this niche with a moisture-swollen barrel cactus.

COURTESY OF VALLEY OF FIRE STATE PARK

*Rainstorms are infrequent events in these drought-prone regions. But in this land of contrasts rains are often torrential. Within moments, the desert soil and rock are saturated. Excess water pours over the land and creates flash floods. Water leaps headlong from cliffs and roars down desert washes. Roads disintegrate; boulders tumble about in the brown, churning waters; and a new landscape results. To witness a desert flash flood is to observe the powerful forces of erosion in action, and it may be a once-in-a-lifetime experience.*

seeds in one area do not all bloom at the same time. A seed reserve is held in the soil to avoid the possible tragedy of an adverse climatic condition that might destroy all the seedlings. Usually, however, once the seed has germinated, it will complete plant development and produce at least one new seed. If conditions become unfavorable after germination, the mature plant and flower may be extremely small because they have used all their meager resources to reach the flowering stage. These small plants are often called "belly flowers" because the observer must lie on this part of the anatomy in order to study them closely.

Early spring wildflowers usually produce seeds just prior to the heat and drought of summer. What is to prevent catastrophe if late spring or early summer rains remove the growth inhibitors from the new seed coats and germination begins too soon? Many resourceful annuals have developed a further strategy to prevent just such a potentially suicidal summer germination. They require a period of cold before they will germinate!

Some annuals in drainages have evolved their own techniques to determine the proper level of moisture. They develop hard seed coats. Heavy rains cause flash floods that tumble and abrade the seeds. This breaks the hard coatings, allowing germination to take place at a time when the washes contain the most moisture.

Desert conditions are extreme. The measures taken by the plants to survive this environment are also extreme—and fascinating.

COURTESY OF VALLEY OF FIRE STATE PARK

*This is the only Nevada home of the Utah yucca.*

JEFF GNASS

*The giant four o'clock is a showy spring flower. The beautiful flowers have an interesting arrangement of sepals that simulate petals.*

COURTESY OF VALLEY OF FIRE STATE PARK

*Paper-flower explodes into vibrant color.*

## Animal Adaptations

One of the best animal adaptations to fluctuating desert conditions is that of bearing young during the most favorable time of the year for survival success. Desert bighorn sheep bear their young from January to March. This is the most favorable time to take advantage of the winter and spring annual plants. The bighorn, therefore, are dependent upon late fall rains to assure sufficient forage for feeding lambs. Dry years result in high mortality rates for the young.

Some small rodents may require green vegetation to produce sufficient milk to nurture their young. Dry years will result in greatly reduced infant survival.

Another important animal strategy is to avoid competition over food or space with other animals. Each animal develops a niche within the ecosystem. As an example, one species of insect may lay eggs only on the leaves or stems of a particular plant species, whereas other insects require different plants. Or a certain animal species will feed only on a particular plant or assemblage of plants. Some animals require different heights of plants for their survival. For instance, different species of desert spiders spin webs at different elevations above the ground; or different bird species nest on the desert floor or at varying heights above the ground. Consequently, the greater the variety of plants in a region, or plants of differing heights, the greater the variety of animals.

A niche may also be defined on the basis of food size. Some rodents select smaller seeds than do other rodents. Some species of bats are highly selective in the sizes of insects they eat.

An additional way to divide scarce resources is to physically avoid competitors by being active during a different time of day. A few desert animals, such as lizards, most birds, ground squirrels, and bighorn sheep, are on the "day shift." Others, the *crepuscular* animals, prefer dawn or sunset; they include smaller bats and some species of rodents. Most desert animals are nocturnal.

Desert animals have a strategy for survival not available to plants; they can move. If vegetation is more luxuriant in another area, or prey species are more common elsewhere, they can move to the better environment. The extreme of such movement is exhibited by birds, some of which migrate totally out of the region during the winter, when many plants or insects are dormant.

*Gila Monsters, with their beadlike scales of black with yellow, orange, or pink, are active primarily at dusk and after dark. In the heat of the day they seek the coolness under rocks or in tunnels they dig themselves.*

*Many animals live in Valley of Fire, but most are unseen. The nocturnal mode is a natural adaptation to avoid the heat of a desert day. At night they emerge and scamper about the desert floor. Dawn finds their tracks imprinted in the sand. Here they have wandered between the green seedlings and last year's dried skeletons of the desert primrose. It is a challenge to decipher the behavior of these creatures by "reading" the clues left in the sand. Soon enough the stories of life and death are covered by windblown sand.*

K. C. DENDOOVEN

The ability to move also results in a very common adaptation of desert reptiles and mammals—a nighttime mode of existence. Since most rodents are nocturnal, they are a primary food source for the larger predators; thus bobcats, foxes, coyotes, ringtailed cats, and owls are most active at night. The desert is usually a quiet place during the heat of the day. Most animals have retired underground to burrows where it is cool and where higher humidity prevents water loss from their bodies. Daylight reveals only tracks and droppings.

There are some desert animals, the pocket gopher for example, that spend most of their life underground. Biologists call such species *fossorial*. The gopher avoids heat and predation and feeds on moist roots or green vegetation near the mouths of its tunnels.

Another method of coping with the desert is by physiological adaptation. Some animals, like kangaroo rats, have developed the ability to produce water from their own metabolic processes. They are thus drought-resistant and can survive between periods of rainfall without drinking. Their predators, such as rattlesnakes, are able to derive water from the body fluids of their prey. In desert country, food webs are complex and usually must accommodate water requirements of plants and animals within their food sources. As an example, the roadrunner seen in August may have just eaten a lizard, which the week before ate an insect, which in April ate a spring annual wildflower, whose seed may have been dormant within the soil for five years.

Another physiological adaptation is the ability to hibernate, or *aestivate,* in a torpid state. During the winter months, when there is less green vegetation and there are fewer insects or mammals, some desert bats, rodents, and reptiles lie below the desert surface awaiting the arrival of spring. Some animals are able to aestivate at any time of the year when food is scarce. The desert tortoise and the chuckwalla, a large lizard, use this technique. Some ground squirrels and pocket

RUSS GRATER

RUSS GRATER

The sighting of a majestic bighorn sheep is always a treat for visitors.

mice aestivate through the summer and thus avoid the heat.

Birds are common within the park, and a great number of species may be observed. The birds receive most of their water supply from their foods: insects, fruits, or—in the case of predators—body tissues. Some species are resident only during the cool seasons and migrate either to higher elevations or northward to avoid summer heat and drought.

Like man, desert animals are high enough on the food webs that their survival is largely predicated on the ability of plants to survive. Ingenuity and mobility have allowed man and other animals to adapt to arid conditions.

SUGGESTED READING


DODGE, NATT N. *Flowers of the Southwest Deserts.* 10th ed. Globe, Arizona: Southwest Parks and Monuments Association, 1980.

GRATER, RUSSELL K. *Snakes, Lizards & Turtles of the Lake Mead Region.* Globe, Arizona: Southwest Parks and Monuments Association, 1981.

KRUTCH, JOSEPH WOOD. *The Voice of the Desert.* New York: William Sloane Associates, 1967.

MUNZ, PHILIP A. *California Desert Wildflowers.* Berkeley: University of California Press, 1962.

OLIN, GEORGE. *Mammals of the Southwest Deserts.* Globe, Arizona: Southwest Parks and Monuments Association, 1982.


BILL FIERO

*All desert creatures must adapt to the arid environment. The kit fox is primarily nocturnal to avoid summer heat. Creosote bushes are spaced to avoid competition for water.*

# Man in the Valley

It seems incredible that human beings not only survived these barren desert conditions but developed a culture here as well. This is an environment of extremes. Summer temperatures commonly exceed 105 degrees Fahrenheit in the shade, yet snows often blanket the higher mountains after winter storms. Freezing conditions may extend even to the valley floors. Rainfall averages between four and five inches a year, but desert cloudbursts and flash floods are not uncommon. Strong winds blow during any season. Surely such an environment would test the skills and fortitude of the most ingenious. Indeed, humans could and did meet the challenge. The story of man in Valley of Fire covers millennia and the evolution of many cultures. Who were these people, and how did they cope with the rigors of climate and terrain?

Lost in the eons of prehistory is the moment when mankind first entered this region. Some archaeologists believe the first people arrived more than 15,000 years ago during the latter part of the great glacial age. Evidence of such antiquity is scattered and unproved. Although the great ice sheets never did reach southern Nevada, cool, moisture-laden winds from the receding glaciers blew southward into the area. The landscape was then covered with profuse vegetation; today's dry washes were flowing streams of cool water; and herds of elk, deer, and antelope grazed the valleys. Native horses and camels may have been present, for their bones have been unearthed, along with artifacts of an early people, in excavations to the west of Valley of Fire.

Most archaeologists would agree that humans were in the region 4,000 years ago, a time when the climate was wetter and cooler than today. During this time bighorn sheep were particularly abundant. Gradually the human population grew.

The people who lived in this area during the Gypsum period from 2000 B.C. until 300 B.C. were organized into small groups called nuclear families. Each group consisted of two to four men who, with their wives and children, roamed among favorite hunting areas. The men were primarily responsible for the ambushing and killing of bighorn sheep, the most important food source. The major weapon used by the men was the *atlatl* (AT-latl), a notched stick used to increase the accuracy and distance of a thrown spear. Stone knives were used for killing and skinning game. The women and children caught rabbits, tortoises,

K. C. DENDOOVEN

*This carving, patiently chipped into rock by a Native American artist centuries ago, portrays an ancient hunting implement, the atlatl, and the bighorn sheep hunted with it.*

*"The Cabins," built by Civilian Conservation Corps workers in the 1930s, blend into the natural surroundings from which the sandstone building materials were derived.*

GAIL BANDINI

*Petroglyphs adorn many of the desert-varnished rock faces in the park. The meaning of this artwork is not understood by scientists, but its artistry can be appreciated by all.*

and other reptiles and collected and prepared wild plant food to supplement their diet. Their principal tools were digging sticks and baskets. They also used milling stones, called *metates* (meh-TAH-teys), on which they ground plant foods. The families used the hides and body parts of bighorn sheep for clothes, blankets, and coverings for their huts. Use of Valley of Fire was probably shared by two to five such nuclear families, who traveled to the Valley periodically to camp near a water source and to hunt and gather. After the bighorn sheep population had declined from overhunting, or when the animals had become wary of the hunters, the nuclear families abandoned the temporary base camps. Once the animals repopulated the area, the people returned.

During periods when game was abundant there was considerable leisure time. The Gypsum-period peoples used some of this time to create elaborate rock art, known as petroglyphs, that still adorns the rocks of the park. Carefully pecked into the black desert-varnish surfaces of the sandstone are geometric designs, bighorn sheep, the atlatl, and numerous tracks and animal forms.

Toward the end of the Gypsum period, population levels increased slowly. Simultaneously, climatic conditions deteriorated as the weather became warmer and drier. Gradually the culture adapted to these changed conditions. Archaeologists refer to this cultural response as the Moapa and Muddy River phases, and they place the time span from 300 B.C. to A.D. 700.

Hunters, formerly dependent mainly upon big game, now pursued small game such as rabbits, ground squirrels, lizards, and birds. Mule deer and desert bighorn were hunted to augment the menu. The gathering of wild plants became increasingly important in maintaining a subsistence. This shift in economic emphasis created a greater reliance on the riparian, or stream, areas. Here in a rich biotic community were the roots, seeds, tubers, and berries necessary to sustain life. The people settled in the valleys of the Virgin and Muddy rivers to the northeast of Valley of Fire. These inhabitants lived in pits covered by a network of sticks and mud that served as their homes.

Occasionally hunters would pursue bighorn in Valley of Fire, but food was too scarce to permit long periods of occupancy. The hunters would carry meat and hides back to their families living along the Virgin and Muddy rivers. These Moapa-

and Muddy River-phase hunters were also ritualistic and were probably responsible for some of the petroglyphs found in the Valley.

The atlatl was still used during the early part of this period, but it was eventually replaced by the bow and arrow. This new weapon was easier to carry and more accurate, and it allowed repeat shots within a shorter time.

With increasing dependence upon plant food, risks of survival became fewer than in earlier big-game hunting days. Population expanded, however, placing greater pressure on food sources. These demands caused a decline in availability of small game and also forced people to move to areas that were less productive of plant foods. But a new discovery—farming—created an even more dramatic change in their culture. This new development probably had its origin in Mexico or South America and was brought to the southern Nevada area by migrating peoples. There is no evidence of hostility between the newcomers, the *Anasazi* (Ah-nah-SAH-zee), and earlier inhabitants. These new farmers began to cultivate corn and squash. Storage of foods also became necessary to carry them through lean times. It was more efficient to carry the food to the people than to have the people pursue the food.

Knowledge of farming has the natural effect of decreasing dependency on gathering and hunting for food. No longer did nuclear families have to live a free-roaming, nomadic existence in search of seasonal wild plants or large game. These early Anasazi people, often referred to as the Basketmakers, grew their corn, squash, and beans near their villages along the riparian bottomlands of the Muddy and Virgin rivers. It now became more efficient to work in larger groups. Extended families lived near each other to assist in large rabbit drives or to help with the harvesting. Influential leaders of the groups exercised more decision making.

How do we know these things about a culture so ancient? It is a puzzle pieced together from the evidence, far from mute, that they left behind. Animal bones reveal the type of game they hunted. Metates attest to the importance of wild plant food in their diets. The kinds of plants can be identified by seeds and by plant fibers that had caught in woven baskets or that had left impressions on pottery.

The innovation of basketry significantly changed the capabilities of these industrious people to utilize their natural resources. Remnants of baskets woven from plant fibers indicate the development of this most useful and important piece of material culture. Some of their baskets were woven so tightly they could have held water; hot stones dropped into water in these containers could have boiled their foods. These ancient folk also wove mats, trays, sandals, and hunting nets.

Around A.D. 300 the Basketmakers learned how to use clay to make sun-dried cookware. This technique was gradually refined into pottery making, an art that played an important role in transforming the culture of the farming Basketmakers into the more highly organized, ritualized society known as the Lost City and Mesa House peoples.

Around A.D. 700, at the beginning of the period archaeologists refer to as the Lost City and Mesa House phases, a significant event occurred. The increasing population of farmers discovered they were not alone in this region. There is evidence to indicate that Lower Colorado Yuman peoples migrated into the area from the south. There is also evidence to support the migration of Numic people, the Paiute, at about A.D. 900.

K. C. DENDOOVEN

*Creative Indian artisans combined beauty with function. This pottery reflects the culture and lifestyle of the ancient ones. The carefully crafted pot may have been used for storing kernels of corn, or perhaps water, in an ancient pueblo.*

Economic competition over critical food resources probably occurred between the earlier inhabitants and these new arrivals. To make matters worse, as competition increased and Lost City–phase population grew, climatic conditions worsened.

To cope with these new conditions the Lost City residents increasingly shifted toward an agricultural economy with an even greater emphasis on stored resources. Double cropping and irrigation were utilized in the riverine areas.

NORMA ENGBERG

*The desert tortoise was an important food source for the Anasazi. For the tortoise the beavertail cactus is a major plant food. The food webs of the desert are often complex. Such complexity aids in the survival of species.*

Initially the Lost City–phase people used Valley of Fire much as did those of the Moapa and Muddy River phases. The barren, rocky expanse of Valley of Fire could not support the villages of Anasazi farmers dependent upon water for crops. However, as conditions worsened, hunting trips to the Valley probably increased. The bighorn population must have decreased sharply as a result of overhunting. The hunters increasingly turned their attention to other resources, such as rabbits, tortoises, and small reptiles, as well as bighorn sheep. The hunters continued to occupy the same camp sites as had their ancestors. They probably contributed to the rock art. They also carried food supplies back to their homes in the river valleys. Toward the end of this period, women probably accompanied men to help collect plants and seeds. As increasing numbers of Paiutes hunted the Valley, Mesa House–phase people abandoned hunting and gathering in Valley of Fire and concentrated on their farming in the river valleys.

The inhabitants increasingly aggregated into larger villages, or *pueblos* (PWAY-blows), consisting of 20 or more residential units. These Pueblo people relied more heavily on trade—exporting turquoise, salt, ceramics, and perhaps cotton blankets and importing shell beads, ceramics, obsidian, and food. As climatic conditions worsened and population continued to grow, exchange became increasingly important. Trade partners included other Anasazi groups to the east and south as well as Yuman and Numic peoples. On a regional basis, social units became more integrated. Complex tribal-level organization of the society created village leaders capable of representing their constituents.

New architectural styles either evolved or were imported, and pueblos of adobe and rock were built alongside the underground pithouses to serve as homes.

The primary centers of Anasazi culture were to the east, in the plateau country of Arizona, New Mexico, Utah, and Colorado. People living near Valley of Fire in the Muddy and Virgin river valleys were on the cultural periphery. They were, in a sense, "country cousins" of the highly developed cultures at Mesa Verde and Chaco Canyon to the east. Artifacts and reconstructions of pithouses and pueblos are preserved in an excellent display at the Lost City Museum in Overton, a few miles northeast of the park.

About A.D. 1150 the Anasazi abandoned the region. Theories to explain this exodus are heatedly debated by southwestern archaeologists. Some argue that a combination of increasing population, competition, and a prolonged drought around 1150 caused the residents to abandon marginal areas of their culture and emigrate to more productive agricultural lands. The tribal-level organization established intergroup contact, which allowed fusion of the Nevada Anasazi with groups who lived on better farmlands elsewhere. This migration left Valley of Fire to the Southern Paiute culture.

The Paiute had already adapted to the desert. Unfettered by accoutrements of extensive farming and village life, they existed in close ecological balance with the arid land. Population density was low. Small family groups, engaged in hunting and gathering, lived a nomadic life following seasonal harvests, just as the earliest inhabitants of the Desert culture had done 10,000 years before. The Mojave Desert supports few

The Lost City Museum, a state museum a few miles northeast of the park, in Overton, Nevada, contains an excellent collection of pottery and other artifacts from many different Indian cultures of the region. A reconstructed pueblo and ceremonial kiva also allow visitors to experience an Anasazi lifestyle.

K. C. DENDOOVEN

plants in any one area, so the foragers moved extensively and could not become dependent upon stored foods. Because plants ripened at different times, the Paiute relied on a great variety rather than on a single or a few species. Variations in elevation provide different plant habitats and thus greatly increase the number of edible species available to a foraging people. Paiute subsistence strategy relied on both spatial and altitude variations to yield sufficient food resources for survival.

In Valley of Fire there is a wide altitude range, hence the area was ideally suited for Paiute occupancy. The Paiute were seasonal users of the land, with their times of occupation controlled by the maturing cycles of their food plants. There were no permanent or even long-term campsites within Valley of Fire. Consequently, there were no known families or bands of Paiutes specifically identified with the Valley. Rather, there was joint use by many Paiutes. Highest seasonal use was probably in spring, when water would stand in depressions and edible plants would be in greatest abundance.

Paiute families generally had a customary division of duties. Women gathered plants, made baskets, cooked, and cared for young children. Men hunted big game, made tools, tanned hides, and handled health matters. Building houses, car-

DAN MAST

The desert appears barren of food to many Valley of Fire visitors. To the earlier Native American inhabitants, however, it was a veritable supermarket of various foods. Much of their extensive knowledge of foods and medicines is known today and yields a means of survival for knowledgeable desert dwellers should they become lost or stranded. The beans of this catclaw acacia are edible and may be ground into flour for bread.

K. C. DEN DOOVEN

*These baskets were woven by Paiute Indians early in this century, except for the* olla *(OH-yah), or jar, on the left, which dates from prehistoric times. In their techniques of basket construction the Paiute closely resemble their ancestors the Basket Makers.*

K. C. DEN DOOVEN

rying family goods, fetching water, and hunting small game were done by both men and women.

What was it like to be a Paiute in this area? For food gathering and collecting water, tightly woven baskets were used. Clay pottery was utilized occasionally for cooking. To kill big game they made use of the bow and arrow and fashioned projectile points from stone. Plant food was ground on metates. They constructed huts of brush and sometimes thatched them for winter warmth. Rock shelters and shaded sites made suitable summer homes. The Paiute were well adapted to their environment.

Social organization among the Paiute was simple. The nuclear family was the unit of both producing and consuming. Each group had a leader who helped make decisions regarding camp movements or selection of gathering areas. This person had no power to coerce his family, but led by wisdom, example, and persuasion. Individuals had freedom of choice. The other prominent figure was the shaman, who had rapport with supernatural beings. He was valuable to the group in medical affairs and in foretelling events.

The Paiute believed that the land would supply their needs. Their simple yet efficient technology, coupled with hard work, did indeed furnish them with an adequate standard of living. Their way of life was harmonious with the environment and asked nothing of it beyond its ability to provide. But it did require of them great skill and knowledge for survival. These, then, were the people the early explorers and settlers found living in Valley of Fire when they first entered the area.

### The Europeans Arrive

The famous mountain man Jedediah Smith led the first party of fur trappers into the area in 1826. This initial contact of Indian and European cultures was amicable. During the 1830s and 1840s traders and travelers from Santa Fe followed Smith's route along the Virgin River. This trail, known as the Spanish Trail, passed to the east of Valley of Fire or took a shortcut along the western boundary of the park. Kit Carson traveled the area several times in the 1840s.

*Deciduous trees are rare in Valley of Fire. A lone cottonwood receives moisture from deep below the sands of a desert wash. Cottonwoods were a welcome sight for early desert travelers. Their presence indicates water; their canopy provides shade.*

*The terrain traversed by early Europeans is rugged and difficult to cross. There was little shelter, food, or water for either the immigrants or their stock. Rocks broke wagonwheels, heat parched tongues, and hunger plagued travelers.*

In the latter part of this decade a dramatic change took place in the use of the route to the west of the park. The number of travelers greatly increased, and the new immigrants came via Salt Lake City rather than Santa Fe. The Spanish Trail, used mostly in the winter months by pack trains, became the Mormon Road and was used mostly by wagon trains. This was the main route through the region to California until the coming of the railroad in the early twentieth century. After the Treaty of Guadalupe Hidalgo ceded land from Mexico in 1848, southern Nevada, including Valley of Fire, became part of the United States.

The arrival of European culture was traumatic to the Paiute. Although there were occasional hostilities between immigrants and Paiutes, often over the ownership of animals, the greatest impact on the Paiute was from farmers who believed in private property. Beginning in 1864, Mormon colonists settled along the Muddy River, adjacent to the park. They soon displaced the Paiute from the Muddy and Virgin river valleys. The newcomers diverted river and spring water for intensive irrigation agriculture. The delicate balance of numerous resources, required for the Paiute way of life, was destroyed with the usurpation of the most productive riparian environments.

The Paiute did not resist with force the incursions of the pioneers. Instead, the Indians employed a pattern of harassment, theft, and annoyance. They were attracted to the material goods, stock, and crops of the settlers. To attain

DAVID MUENCH

*The sculpted recesses and hollows that so appeal to the artistic imagination of today's visitors must have also had other significance for earlier humans. Such shadowed overhangs meant vital sheltered respite from the heat of the midday summer sun or refuge within a protected recess from winter's cold northerly winds. Plans for a morning hunt or an evening ceremonial were almost certainly born in this place, Perhaps the illustrious fugitive Mouse hid here from a pursuing posse.*

these items Paiutes became involved in seasonal agricultural employment. Wages, often paid in goods, were usually too little to support a family. Consequently, traditional hunting and gathering continued.

In 1872 the Moapa Indian Reservation was established along the Muddy River; about 300 people live there today. There are about 72,000 acres on the reservation, and most families live in modern frame houses or trailers. The tribal council administers a farm and several businesses. Little of the original material culture survives, but the Paiute take pride in their Native American philosophies and attitudes.

Present-day agriculture in the Muddy River Valley utilizes extensive irrigation methods and improved fertilizers that allow progressively more intense farming. In the past, some stock grazing of desert land did occur, but it was always marginal. Most grazing is now located in the river valleys.

Valley of Fire is surrounded by mineral resources. Since prehistoric days salt has been mined southeast of the park. There are gypsum mines to the west and north. Magnesite and silica mining operations are located to the east. To the south lie borates and beds rich in lithium. Silica sands within the park might have been exploited except the sand was too fine and transportation to California markets was too expensive. Fortuitously, Valley of Fire did not contain commercial mineral deposits and thus was spared from large-scale mining activites.

## Mouse's Tank

Much has been said and written of Mouse, a Paiute Indian whom legend has branded an outlaw. There are many versions of what created Mouse's problems with the settlers, but there is a general lack of historical documentation. Some say Mouse caused no trouble to the Indian community in which he grew up, while others claim that some Indians feared and hated him. One version states that Mouse first had trouble with a farmer who refused to pay him for work done. Another alleges that he had stolen some vegetables from the garden of a farmer who then shot at him. Still another story attests that the trouble began in January 1897 at Bonelli's Landing. George Bonelli, a merchant and rancher, employed Mouse as a hand on a ferry that crossed the Colorado River. Mouse became drunk and shot up an Indian camp with his pistol. Bonelli and his men disarmed him and locked him up for the evening. He was fired from his job and ferried across the river to Arizona. There he reportedly killed two prospectors.

Several intensive searches were conducted for Mouse, but he successfully eluded capture. During these hunts he supposedly used the rugged terrain of Valley of Fire for a hideout. Here he would sometimes use "Mouse's Tank," a depression in the rock that catches and holds rainwater for a time after intense rainstorms. It is well hidden within the labyrinth of rock formations on the floor of Petroglyph Canyon and is a favorite attraction for park visitors. On July 6, 1897, Mouse is reported to have raided the garden of an Indian woman. A posse formed and tracked him through Valley of Fire. On the morning of July 11 they sighted Mouse near Muddy Spring and ordered him to surrender. Mouse apparently shot at his pursuers, who, after an hour-long running fight, shot and killed him.

### SUGGESTED READING


Euler, Robert C. *Southern Paiute Ethnohistory.* Salt Lake City: University of Utah Anthropological Papers, No. 78, 1966.

Ruppert, David E. *Lake Mead National Recreation Area; An Ethnographic Overview.* Tucson, Arizona: Western Archaeological and Conservation Center Publications in Anthropology, No. 3, 1976.

Shutler, Richard, Jr., and Mary E. Shutler. *Archaeological Survey in Southern Nevada.* Carson City: Nevada State Museum Anthropological Papers, No. 7, 1962.

Shutler, Richard, Jr., et al. *Lost City, Pueblo Grande de Nevada.* Carson City: Nevada State Museum Anthropological Papers, No. 5, 1961.

Wormington, H. M. *Prehistoric Indians of the Southwest.* Denver: Denver Museum of Natural History, Popular Series No. 7, [1947] 1973.

BRUCE KAPLAN

*Here on the floor of Petroglyph Canyon is the water hole, or tank, that legend says supplied Mouse. This Paiute Indian, considered an outlaw by contemporary settlers, traveled through this area and reputedly hid in the labyrinth of canyons in Valley of Fire. In 1897 he was shot and killed by a posse.*

*Following Pages: Red sandstones contrast with blue water and gray mountains. Photo by Willard Clay*

K. C. DENDOOVEN

# *Petroglyphs—Writings in the Desert*

A constant source of fascination and speculation to archaeologists and park visitors are the many petroglyphs pecked into boulders and joint faces throughout Valley of Fire. Geometric and naturalistic designs are preserved in these ancient pieces of rock art, the most prominent—and startling—reminders of earlier cultures in existence. The most numerous design elements used by ancient artists and the most interesting to modern observers are the desert bighorn and human forms.

No adequate technique has been developed to date petroglyphs accurately. Thus their ages and the cultures responsible for them are not definitely known. The atlatl pecked into a joint face of Aztec sandstone at Atlatl Rock has been interpreted as dating from the early cultures that began to use this weapon, as long ago as 3,000 years. Other archaeologists believe most of the petroglyphs are the work of the Anasazi, who departed the area in A.D. 1150. They are probably the work of all the early peoples who visited Valley of Fire.

What do they mean? Some petroglyphs may have been used in hunting or religious rituals. Others appear to be maps, historical records, accounts of successful hunts, clan or personal marks, or directions for finding water. Experts are not in agreement as to their meanings. Some believe they are merely the idle scratching of hunters relieving the boredom of a hot afternoon; others consider them important hieroglyphics, perhaps the key to a lost language. But in spite of the controversy and mystery surrounding their origins and true meanings, there can be no doubt that petroglyphs are an important link to past cultures. Through their presence modern man has been given the gift of insight into the sensitivity and art of a truly remarkable people—a people highly skilled in their understanding of and adaptation to a seemingly hostile and uninhabitable environment.

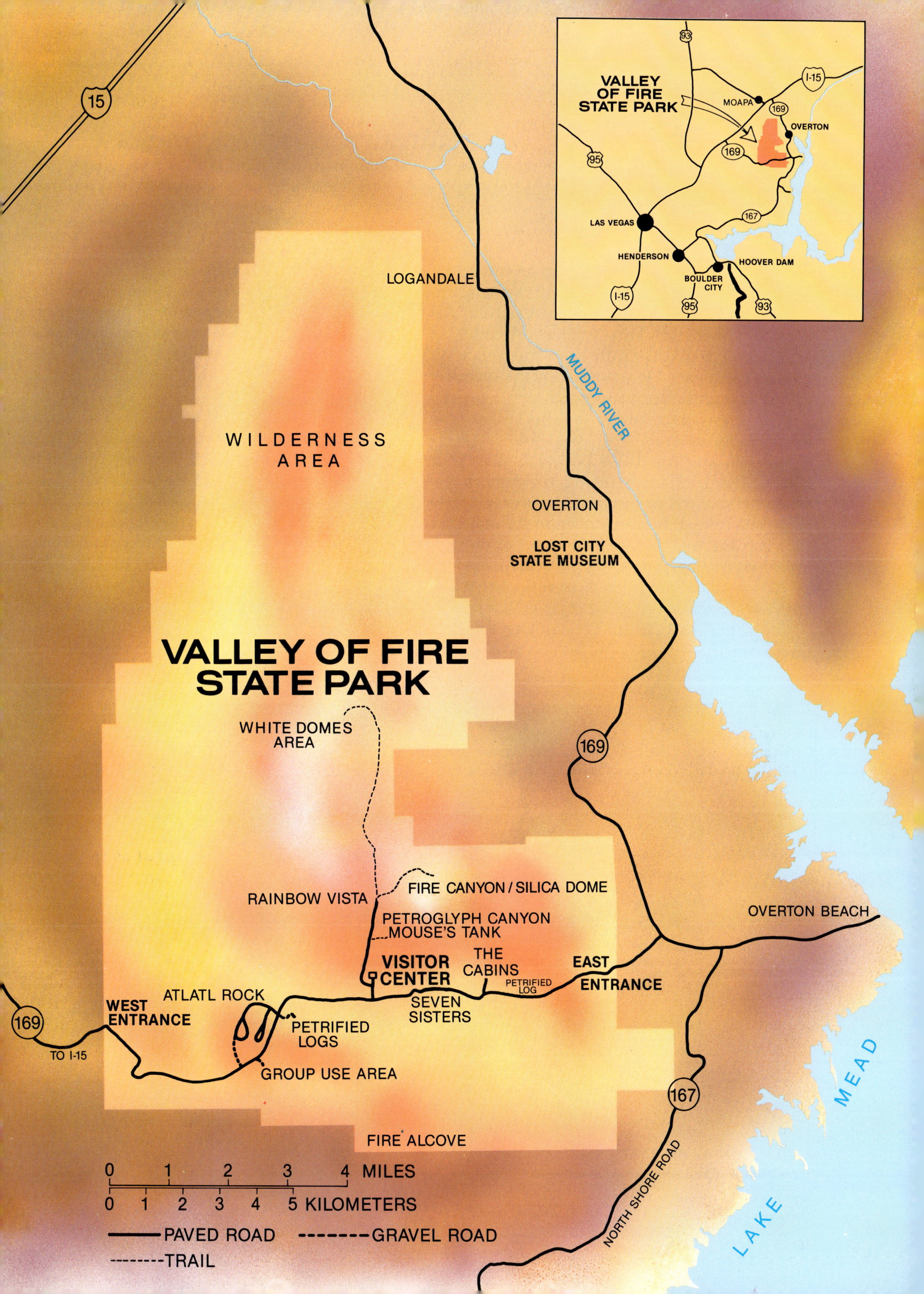

VALLEY OF FIRE STATE PARK
MOAPA
OVERTON
LAS VEGAS
HENDERSON
BOULDER CITY
HOOVER DAM
I-15
93
95
169
167
15
LOGANDALE
MUDDY RIVER
WILDERNESS AREA
OVERTON
LOST CITY STATE MUSEUM
VALLEY OF FIRE STATE PARK
WHITE DOMES AREA
169
RAINBOW VISTA
FIRE CANYON / SILICA DOME
PETROGLYPH CANYON
MOUSE'S TANK
VISITOR CENTER
THE CABINS
PETRIFIED LOG
EAST ENTRANCE
OVERTON BEACH
WEST ENTRANCE
ATLATL ROCK
PETRIFIED LOGS
SEVEN SISTERS
169
TO I-15
GROUP USE AREA
167
FIRE ALCOVE
NORTH SHORE ROAD
LAKE MEAD
0 1 2 3 4 MILES
0 1 2 3 4 5 KILOMETERS
PAVED ROAD
GRAVEL ROAD
TRAIL

## *Establishing a Park*

During the late nineteenth century, or perhaps the early years of the twentieth, Valley of Fire became a cutoff on the wagon road to Las Vegas. Clark County built a rough road through the Valley in 1914 to serve as part of the Arrowhead Trail between Salt Lake City and Los Angeles. By 1925 this route was abandoned in favor of the more northerly route followed by today's Interstate 15. According to legend an important Valley of Fire event occurred prior to the abandoning of this portion of the Arrowhead Trail. In the 1920s an official of the American Automobile Association was driving through the Valley on this road at sunset. He was awed by the spectacle of red rays diffused on red rock and later described the whole valley as "on fire." Hence the name, Valley of Fire.

Also during the 1920s Nevada's Governor James Scrugham, recognizing the remarkable beauty of the Valley, requested transfer of the land from federal public domain to the state. By 1931 Nevada was deeded 8,700 acres of the Valley. From this beginning the park had increased by 1975 to 42,000 acres. It will eventually encompass over 56,000 acres.

From 1933 to 1935 the Civilian Conservation Corps constructed roads and buildings in the valley, including the stone shelters at "The Cabins" site. The work in Nevada was supervised by Colonel Thomas W. Miller, who later was instrumental in the creation of a state park here.

In 1935 the Nevada legislature, responding to local concerns and pressures of southern Nevadans, officially established the State Park Commission. In that year Valley of Fire was designated Nevada's first state park.

Valley of Fire can be seen and enjoyed from your car, but it is a far more fulfilling experience to travel as much of the area as you can on foot. Whether taking a day hike into White Domes or Fire Canyon or a five-minute stroll from the road, the opportunity to observe the natural wonders surrounding you requires the use of all the senses. Smell the pungent odor of the creosote and touch the coarse surfaces of rock. Hear the song of the canyon wren echoing from the sheer walls. Think of the vast span of time recorded in rock, and of the ancient peoples who patiently chipped their art into the rock surfaces. They were in harmony with their natural surroundings, and they survived. Consider the life you lead, and reflect that parks such as Valley of Fire—necessary for the preservation of nature—may also be, as Thoreau observed,"... in wildness ... preservation of man."

*The modern visitor center is designed to blend into the surrounding desert.*

GAIL BANDINI

*Inside back cover: Sandstone forms by David Muench*

*Back cover: Sandstone monolith by Jeff Gnass*



Printed by Dong-A Printing and Publishing, Seoul, Korea